Pebble
Plus

Exploring the Galaxy

Mars

by Thomas K. Adamson

Consulting Editor: Gail Saunders-Smith, PhD

Consultant: James Gerard
Aerospace Education Specialist, NASA
Kennedy Space Center, Florida

CAPSTONE PRESS
a capstone imprint

Pebble Plus is published by Capstone Press,
151 Good Counsel Drive, P.O. Box 669, Mankato, Minnesota 56002.
www.capstonepub.com

042010
005760

Library of Congress Cataloging-in-Publication Data
Adamson, Thomas K., 1970–
    Mars / by Thomas K. Adamson.—Rev. and updated.
    p. cm.—(Pebble plus. Exploring the galaxy)
    Includes bibliographical references and index.
    ISBN-13: 978-1-4296-0737-7 (hardcover)
    ISBN-13: 978-1-4296-5811-9 (saddle-stitched)
    1. Mars (Planet)—Juvenile literature. I. Title. II. Series.
QB641.A33 2008
523.43—dc22   2007004452

Summary: Simple text and photographs describe the planet Mars.

Editorial Credits
Mari C. Schuh, editor; Kia Adams, designer; Alta Schaffer, photo researcher

Photo Credits
Digital Vision, 5 (Venus), 19, 20–21
NASA, 6–7, 8–9, 17; JPL, 5 (Jupiter), JPL/Caltech, 5 (Uranus), JPL/Malin Space Science Systems, 15
PhotoDisc Inc., cover, 4 (Neptune), 5 (Earth, Sun, Mars, Mercury, Saturn), 11 (both); PhotoDisc Imaging, 1; Stock Trek, 12–13

Note to Parents and Teachers

The Exploring the Galaxy set supports national science standards related to earth science. This book describes and illustrates the planet Mars. The photographs support early readers in understanding the text. The repetition of words and phrases helps early readers learn new words. This book also introduces early readers to subject-specific vocabulary words, which are defined in the Glossary section. Early readers may need assistance to read some words and to use the Table of Contents, Glossary, Read More, Internet Sites, and Index sections of the book.

Table of Contents

The Red Planet

Mars is the fourth planet

from the Sun.

Mars is called

the red planet.

The Solar System

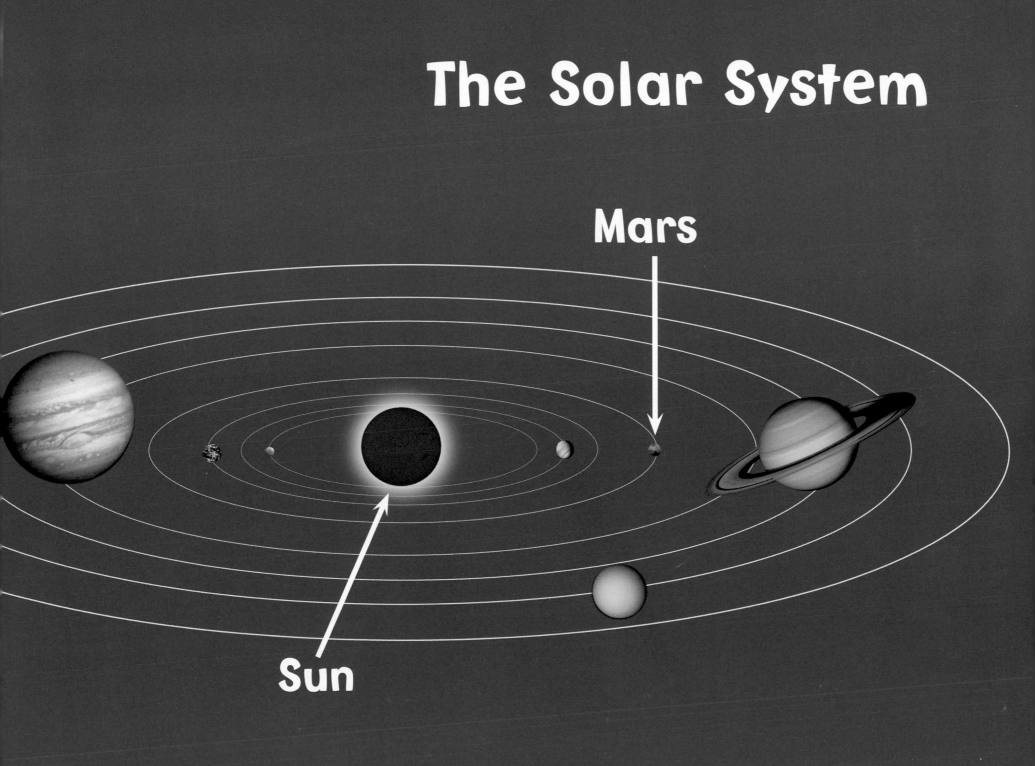

Mars

Sun

The red-brown surface
of Mars is like a desert.
Rocks cover
the dry, dusty land.

Mars has deep canyons
and huge volcanoes.
Mars has ice at its poles.

9

Size of Mars

Mars is smaller than Earth.

Earth is about

twice as wide as Mars.

Earth

Mars

Air and Weather

The air on Mars
is thin and cold.
People could not
breathe the air.

Dust storms
happen often on Mars.
They can cover
the whole planet.

Exploring Mars

A trip to Mars from Earth
takes about six months.
More spacecraft have
explored Mars than
any other planet.

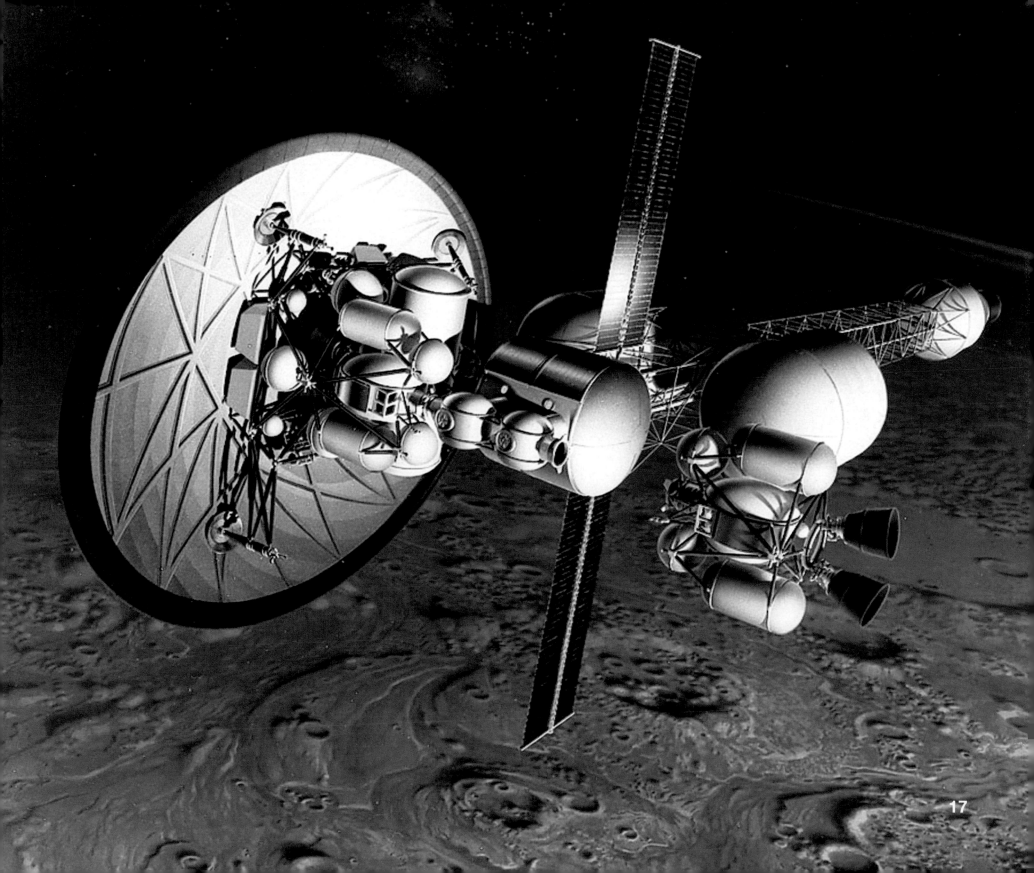

Scientists used a rover
to study rocks and dirt
on Mars.
Scientists controlled
the rover from Earth.

Someday people might
live on Mars.
They would have to wear
space suits and build shelters
that hold air
they can breathe.

21

Glossary

canyon—a long, deep valley with steep sides

crater—a large bowl-shaped hole in the ground

desert—a very dry area of land; deserts are sandy and rocky.

planet—a large object that moves around the Sun; Mars is the fourth planet from the Sun; there are eight planets in the solar system.

pole—the top or bottom part of a planet

rover—a small vehicle that people can move by using remote control; a rover called Sojourner explored Mars.

spacecraft—a vehicle used to travel in space; spacecraft that have traveled to Mars have not included people.

Sun—the star that the planets move around; the Sun provides light and heat for the planets.

volcano—a mountain with vents; melted rock oozes out of the vents; volcanoes on Mars are no longer active.

Read More

Orme, Helen, and David Orme. *Let's Explore Mars.* Space Launch! Milwaukee: Gareth Stevens, 2007.

Richardson, Adele. *Mars.* First Facts: The Solar System. Mankato, Minn.: Capstone Press, 2008.

Wimmer, Teresa. *Mars.* My First Look at Planets. Mankato, Minn.: Creative Education, 2007.

Internet Sites

FactHound offers a safe, fun way to find Internet sites related to this book. All of the sites on FactHound have been researched by our staff.

Here's how:

1. Visit *www.facthound.com*

2. Choose your grade level.

3. Type in this book ID **9781429607377** for age-appropriate sites. You may also browse subjects by clicking on letters, or by clicking on pictures and words.

4. Click on the **Fetch It** button.

FactHound will fetch the best sites for you!

Index

Word Count: 139
Grade: 1
Early-Intervention Level: 15